MASCOT COACHES

and the

VOTIER FAMILY

by

Jill Howard
(formerly Votier)

Published February 2006 by Jill Howard

Design by Holm Oak Publishing
24 Church View, Holton, Halesworth,
Suffolk IP19 8PB
Telephone: 01986 875999

Artwork production by Gatehouse Design
Telephone: 01986 798857

Printed by Barnwell's Print Ltd
Aylsham, Norfolk

British Cataloguing in Publication Data.
A catalogue record for this book is available
from the British Library.

ISBN 0-9533406-3-5

About the Author
JILL ANDREA HOWARD

I was born on 26th March 1943, the youngest child of
Leonard and Hilda Votier, proprietors of MASCOT
Coaches in Norwich. Educated at Lonsdale School
and Norwich City College, I married Rodney Howard
in 1965 and we have a son and daughter and
four grandchildren.

After working as a secretary for a local builder and
as a cook in a stately home, I am now retired and
living with Rodney in Ashby, where I enjoy cooking,
gardening and family history, and also playing with
our grandchildren.

This book is dedicated to my parents and family.

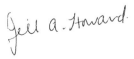

ACKNOWLEDGEMENTS

I should like to express my gratitude to the following people for their help and advice in the making of this book:

Mr A. Braithwaite; Mr E. Bush; Mr R. Burton; Mr D. Cook; Mr W. Nickerson; Mr S. Peacock; Mr Pinnock; Mr K. Rackham; Mr A. Read; Mr R.D. Rowlands; Mr D. Rudd; Mr A. Saunders; Mr G. Semmens; Mr D. Simpson; Mr C. Southwell; Mr G. Twiddy; Mr J. Walker; Mr Weeds; Mr A. Witard; Mr A. Wright; Mr L. Wright.

Also my thanks to Mr Derek James of Eastern Counties Newspapers and Mr Neil Haverson of 'Let's Talk' magazine.

I am deeply grateful to my family for their memories, help and support, without which this book would not have been possible.

CONTENTS

Page

FOREWORD

by Mr A.E. Whitard

I have known the Votier family for over seventy years, from when I used to audit the accounts whilst working for Cecil Howard and Co. of Burlington Buildings in Norwich in the 1930s.

I feel honoured to have been asked to write the foreword to the history of a local family and their unique business, which grew with the family – VOTIER and MASCOT COACHES.

Leonard and Hilda raised three sons and four daughters (only the daughters now survive). The boys drove the coaches (and father of course) as they were added to the fleet, plus one or two part-time drivers.

I could be the only eye-witness still alive to recall the growth of the remarkable business, although there are no doubt several customers who still remember the Sunday coach runs to Kelling Sanatorium, which was the only means by which most people could visit relatives.

Leonard loved playing bowls and donated cups to various leagues in the City which ae still being played for annually. He played at The Falcon public house on Cromer Road, Norwich, and spent the last days of his life a few yards from there.

I am sure you will find the reading and photographs which follow very interesting.

CHAPTER 1
LEONARD AND THE EARLY YEARS

LEONARD VOTIER was born on 20th February, 1902 at 48 Patteson Road, Norwich, in the parish of St. Clement Without – just outside the city walls near Magdalen Gates in Norwich.

He was the youngest son of Benjamin James Votier and Charlotte (nee Clayton) the daughter of William Clayton a coal merchant and publican, and Martha (nee Larkman). They kept the 'Jolly Dyers' Public House in Fishergate in Norwich from 1881 to 1891, where they took in lodgers from the theatre business.

Leonard's father Benjamin had bright ginger hair and the temper to go with it. He was quite tall, with a small framed body and was rather dapper in appearance. In later years, he sported a brown trilby hat and wore 'spats' on his legs.

Charlotte Votier with (clockwise from top left) Leonard, William, Alfred, Herbert, Arthur, Florence, Violet c. 1942.

Benjamin worked in the boot and shoe industry all his adult life. He was very clever with his hands and made fine leather high-fashion boots to a very good standard. He once had premises in Oak Street, Norwich where he made and sold his boots and shoes.

Benjamin was a good husband and father but suffered with his nerves. When he felt under pressure, he would take off, and said he was going to stay with his brother William in London. I wonder what his excuse was when on 8th August 1886 he was caught stealing and was threatened with 12 months imprisonment with hard labour.

Charlotte and Benjamin had eleven children of whom nine survived to maturity. With all these children to bring up and Benjamin not always around, Charlotte had to fend for herself. She took in washing and did various cleaning jobs to gain money to feed her children. There was no family allowance to help in those days. It is little wonder Charlotte gladly accepted help from elsewhere for support for herself and growing family. She met and befriended her landlord, William Fake, a wealthy business man.

Mr. Fake was well known as an Artesian well-sinker and water diviner. Being a widower with several children, he was pleased to set up home with Charlotte at 70 Marlborough Road in 1923. They had a very happy life and it was not until after Benjamin died in 1937 that they actually married. Mr. Fake was a good friend to Charlotte whom he called 'Lottie' and he was kind, generous and loving to his step-children.

Leonard did not enjoy good health as a child, as he had a weak heart. He attended the 'Open air' school in Angel Road, Norwich. This later became the Clare School and is now situated in Colman Road, Norwich.

He left school at the age of 14 years, in 1916, to work as a trainee clicker in the boot and shoe trade like his father.

In accordance with the Factory and Workshop Act of 1901, Leonard's mother Charlotte was required to obtain a permit for him to leave school. It was necessary to obtain permission for a child under the age of 16 years to be employed.

Leonard with Charlotte c.1920

After leaving the boot and shoe trade, Leonard worked as a driver for a Mr. Stevens who was contracted out to the post office. Leonard could be seen driving his little van around Norfolk taking in Aylsham, Hanworth and up to Happisburgh delivering the daily mail.

One evening, whilst returning back home to Norwich he was alarmed at what he thought was a 'ghost' in a field. Not having the luxury of modern lights on his vehicle he had mistaken a white-faced donkey in the field for a 'ghost'. All was revealed when he returned to the area the next day in daylight.

On 23rd December, 1922 Leonard married Hilda Nelson, daughter of William and Sarah Nelson of Heigham, at Norwich Register Office. They set up their first home at 62 Admiralty Road, Great Yarmouth.

I do not know what took Leonard and Hilda to this Norfolk Port.

Leonard with fish van c.1923

Great Yarmouth's prosperity was founded on herring fishing and it was once a leading herring port. Steam drifters took over from sail and they landed record catches. The boats were requisitioned during World War I but later returned. It was about this time in 1923 when Leonard entered this profession when their first child Leonard Owen (nick-named Kipper) was born in June 1923; the birth certificate gave Leonard's profession as a boat owner's chauffeur.

It is not clear who actually owned the boat, but it is likely it was WESTMACOTT LTD whose registered office was in Barrack Street, Great Yarmouth, which was just around the corner from where Leonard and Hilda lived. Leonard drove a Model 'T' Ford van with 'The Fresh Fish Supply Co' sign-written on the side. He delivered to Markets at Norwich, Swaffham and Fakenham. I often wondered if the name MASCOT was an anagram from the name WESTMACOTT. Leonard had an active mind and would often work things out this way. Later on in the book you will find the story of how MASCOT actually got its name.

CHAPTER 2
THE BIRTH OF A BUSINESS

At the beginning of 1924, Leonard, Hilda and their baby son Leonard returned to Norwich. They rented a house at 56 Marlborough Road.

This was a typical Victorian terraced house. There was a staircase going up through the middle of the house leading to three bedrooms. The living room and kitchen took up the ground floor and outside was the toilet – or thunderbox as some might remember.

Bath night was taken in the living room in a galvanised bath. This would be in front of a warm, cosy coal fire – you scorched on the fire side and froze on the other. The order for bathing was parents first and then the children – youngest last!

Leonard and Hilda's second child – Stella May – was born in 1925. By then, Leonard had secured a job as a driver with Messrs. Bush and Twiddy of Croft Works in Sussex Street, Norwich. This company, formed around 1920, was owned by Mr. Edward Bush, a coal dealer who expanded his business to include light haulage and carriage repairs.

Eventually, the company merged with Twiddy's to become motor engineers and body builders. Mr. Eddie Bush of Filby, son of Edward Bush told me they made charabancs from scratch: having their own foundry they made spokes and rims for the wooden wheels. The ash bodies were constructed in the joinery shop and the metal cladding was made in the foundry. They also employed local self-employed people to upholster the seats. The canvas hood would most probably have been made by Hurns in Exchange Street, Norwich.

Whilst working there, Leonard dreamed of owning his own charabanc, rather than driving 'Blue Bell'.

Charabanc 'Blue Bell'

Eventually, he asked the proprietor, Mr. Bush, if he could build a charabanc for a 'customer'. Mr. Bush was keen to learn the name of the mystery customer but Leonard remained reticent, until the job was completed. Then Mr. Bush again enquired about the name that would have to be on the bill and eventually Leonard replied 'MINE'.

Being a man of his word, Mr. Bush did as asked and sold the vehicle to Leonard at a discounted price of £234. This was a charralorry, registered No CL 6919, complete with chassis. Leonard promptly handed in his notice on 20th December, 1924. He was financially backed by the man who had become his step-father, Mr. William Fake. He repaid him within two years, but they continued to trade as Votier and Fake for a further three years until the partnership was dissolved by mutual agreement in 1931.

Postcard showing a charalorry conversion

Leonard was very proud of his new 14 seater Ford lorry-cum-wagonette which converted to an open-top charabanc with a collapsible black canvas rain hood at the rear. You had to stand on running boards to get in the doors. The windscreen was in two sections with a metal bar down the middle. There were no side windows, just canvas curtains – pleasant fresh air in the summer, but not so good in the cold weather.

In the late 1920's, motorised vehicles were not often seen on the streets. Everyone was trying to recover from the effects of World War I. Imagine the look on the children's faces as they played in the street and Leonard came along in this shiny new charabanc. He would climb down, open the door and say 'Jump in, I'll give you a ride to the garage.'

The children would excitedly scramble onto the seats and argue about who was going to sit at the sides so they could dangle their arms over the edge.

Phyllis Hook (now Todd), a neighbour in Marlborough Road told me she can remember being invited to have a ride and as she and the neighbouring children sat on the back seat, they felt very grand and almost like royalty – waving their arms to amazed neighbours, as they trundled slowly up the road. Once at the garage Leonard would say 'out you get! You can walk home now!'

Delusions of grandeur over! It was only about half a mile back to Marlborough Road from the garage on Mousehold, so the children didn't really mind.

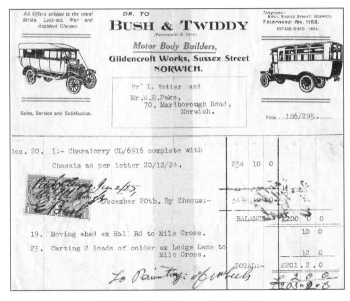

Bush & Twiddy receipt, 1924

Chapter 3
Comfort is the Word

With the departure of Mr. Fake from the business in 1931, a new name was required for the vehicles. Leonard was on a driving job in Swaffham and whilst walking through the Market Place he spotted a shop sign advertising 'Mascot and Norvic' shoes as manufactured by Messrs Howlett and White of Colegate, Norwich. He rather liked the name 'Mascot' and since the England cricket team had been successful that season, he thought he would find a name that made up the initials M.C.C (Marylebone Cricket Club). MASCOT COMFORT COACHES seemed to fit the bill and that is how the name was established.

A few years later, the word 'comfort' was dropped from the title.

Leonard and son Lenny c.1942

Leonard would drive the charalorry by day, mainly carting building materials for repairing aerodrome runways. He would return for tea and a rest whilst Hilda put the babies of the day into the pram, walk to the garage and clean out the vehicle. Leonard would then return to the garage, attach the chara to the lorry chassis and take passengers out for an evening trip.

To start with, this was mainly on Sundays and Bank Holidays. Some typical trips would be: Potter Heigham and Great Yarmouth, Stalham, Happisburgh and North Walsham, or Ranworth Broad and Acle. Each passenger could travel for the princely sum of two shillings (ten pence in today's money).

As trips became more popular, the living room at Marlborough Road had to be divided up to provide a booking office. The telephone number was Norwich 102; this featured on the registration plates of several vehicles in the future, including Leonard's private cars.

Some early contracts included:

A.J. Caley Limited, manufacturers of chocolates and crackers in Norwich. Transporting chocolates to Birmingham and returning with a load of tyres from the Dunlop factory back to Norwich. With only a forward and reverse gear, it was often a struggle for the Model 'T' Ford to negotiate St. James Hill with a full load. My cousin 'Billy' said he often had to get out of the vehicle and help to push it up the hill.

The Steam Packet Company of King Street, Norwich – transporting barrels of glucose syrup and molasses to A.J. Caley of Salhouse Road and returning with tinned crackers for export. It was necessary for the crackers to be in a tin as the contents contained small amounts of chocolate.

Barnards Limited of Salhouse Road, Norwich –
transporting galvanised chain-link fencing and wire
products to Birmingham and again returning with
a load of tyres from the Dunlop factory.

With increasing trade, it was decided to purchase
another vehicle.

This one was supplied by the Waveney Co. Ltd,
Raglan Street, Lowestoft in May 1927. It was a much
more luxurious vehicle for passenger use; this had
such items as cushions and squabs upholstered in
Red Antique rexine. The backs of the seats were
covered with hair carpet and finished off with Nickel
Bead. The hood was covered with Black twill, an
added luxury was rigid side curtains, all for the sum
of £337.13s 6d.

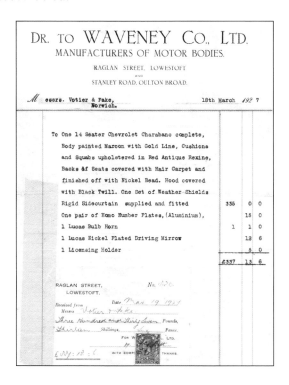

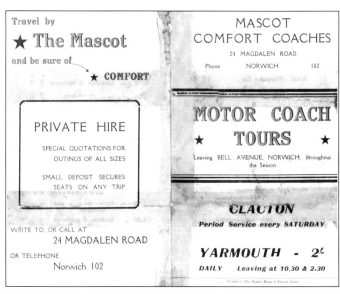

An early Mascot brochure

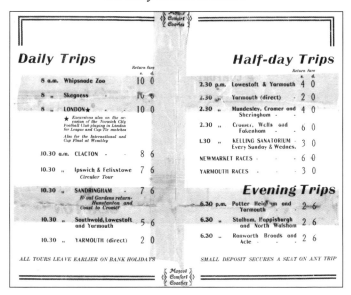

CHAPTER 4
THE FAMILY AND THE FLEET EXPAND

In 1929, the original Ford charabanc was traded in for £95, and this money was used to purchase a Graham chassis from the Norwich Motor Co. Ltd of Recorder Road in Norwich, for £515. Added to this was a 20 seater all-weather coach supplied by Bush and Twiddy. The coach was named 'Little Leonard' after Leonard and Hilda's first born.

In 1930 the Minister of Transport, Herbert Morrison, proposed the passing of a Bill, which duly became the Road Traffic Act 1930. Effective in April 1931, the Act almost overnight brought some semblance of regulated bus and coach services, by requiring any operator wishing to provide or continue to operate a regular public service, to have a licence, stipulating the route and maximum number of vehicles to be operated. It also established the Drivers' Hours Regulations that were to apply, with few changes being made until the introduction of E.E.C. Regulations in the 1970s.

England and Wales were split into ten regions, each of which was controlled by the Traffic commissioners. Mascot were licensed by the Eastern Area at Cambridge.

Applications for journeys were submitted in a white book called 'Notices and Proceedings' and if there were no objections, journeys could then go ahead.

The Road Traffic Act also saw the increase to a maximum speed limit of 30 miles per hour from the previous permitted 20 miles per hour.

On the roadways, tarmacadam was introduced, and in 1934 Percy Shaw of Halifax invented reflective roadstuds – cats eyes as they are more popularly known. They were certainly an improvement for night-time driving.

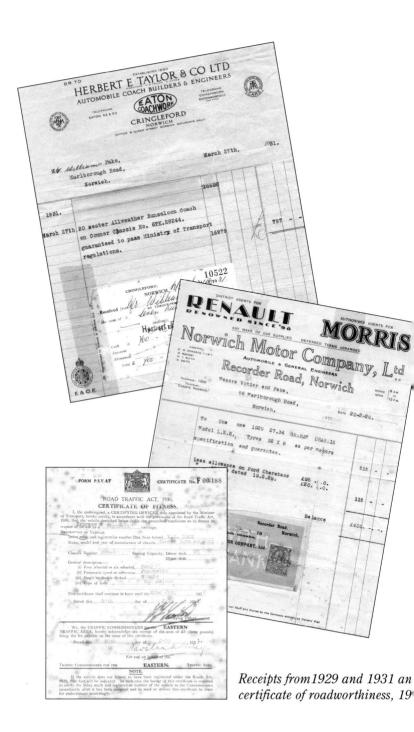

Receipts from 1929 and 1931 an
certificate of roadworthiness, 19

A 1930's outing. Leonard Votier in driver's uniform white coat

All-weather coach on Graham chassis

Church groups, famous for their Sunday School outings, began to hire charabancs for these occasions. Mr. Pinnock, a member of the choir at St. Mary Magdalen church on Silver Road, Norwich told me he remembers going on such an outing to Cromer with Mascot. Lunch and tea would be taken at the Holkham Hotel in Cromer.

The next coach was purchased on the 27th March 1931, a 20 seater all-weather sunsaloon coach, on a Commer Invader chassis, registered No VG 3503 (pictured opposite). This was the last coach bought during the Votier/Fake partnership, from Herbert E. Taylor & Co Ltd. of Cringleford, Norwich, for the sum of £797.

Commer Invader

By 1936, Leonard and Hilda had six children: Leonard Owen, Stella, Eileen, William Edward, Malcolm Reginald and Judy, so a larger house was needed. Number 24 Magdalen Road fitted the bill. This was a five bedroomed, single bay-fronted terrace house with a step from the kitchen into the back yard with an outside toilet and coal shed. The back gate led to a passageway running between Guernsey Road and Stacey Road.

Many happy memories of life at this house include: on Good Friday morning the baker brought round trays, carried on his head, full of freshly baked hot cross buns; a regular delivery of fresh eggs was made by a lady with a large wicker basket; sweets were bought from the corner shop and some favourites included sherbet dip and long strips of liquorice. The milk was delivered fresh daily, transported by horse and cart. The milkman would decant the milk from large galvanised churns by a long-handle ladle, into a variety of containers. There was no thought about sterilisation in those days.

One day, Leonard's love of practical jokes involved an unsuspecting milkman who must have wondered why his horse did not wait whilst he was completing a delivery. From his bedroom window at the front of the house, Leonard urged the horse to 'move on'. When the milkman came out of the house and on to the street – the horse was farther up the road!

Bedford Coach reg. no. SNG 102 at Mile Cross Lane garage c.1956

CHAPTER 5
COPING WITH WORLD WAR II

World War II broke out in 1939. At this time, the living room at Magdalen Road was used for air-raid warden work and was known as ARP Outpost 12.

Hilda and Leonard were both air raid wardens. They helped to distribute all kinds of equipment such as stirrup pumps (portable water pumps) and gas masks from a storeroom at St. Augustine's School.

During the raids, Leonard helped to patrol the roads as well. He would check that 'blackouts' were used at windows and doors at night. Anyone smoking a cigarette whilst walking in the street would soon be told to 'Put out that light'.

Hilda was a volunteer with the WRVS and helped to look after evacuees, sometimes in her own house. She also knitted baby clothes and made nightdresses for those who needed them.

Mascot coach reg. no. WJ 518 c.1938

Although the family had an Andersen shelter in the back yard, this was very small and damp. So the family chose to go to the large communal shelter in Mill Lane, next to St. Paul's Church, for all the local residents. There was a great community spirit amongst the families who gathered there until the 'all clear' sounded.

The coaches were garaged at Sussex Street and because this was rather close to the city centre, it was in danger of being a prime target area during bombing raids. So, for safety reasons, the coaches were 'evacuated' to the country at night. Carrying members of the family, along with close neighbours, the coaches were driven to Felthorpe Woods on the Holt Road.

The drivers would pick up anyone else on the road who had fled on foot. They would all stay in the coaches for the night and return to Norwich when safe to do so.

During one such visit to Felthorpe, Leonard had a chance meeting with a local farmer and landowner whose name was Mr. Broom. After a chat, the Votier family were offered 'lodgings' at the Broom farmhouse with relatively safe parking for the coaches.

The family hold many happy memories of the old farmhouse in the woods.

There was a large cooking range in the kitchen; cream lace curtains at the windows; red chenille table covers under tall glass-chimneyed oil lamps.

To the small children, the beds seemed very tall, with enormous feather mattresses. The two families would sit around the large pine kitchen table playing cards and board games. During the day, the children would play in the woods and help Mrs. Broom to feed the hens and collect up the eggs.

Harvest time was very popular, when all the children would lend a hand and get to ride the horses.

Mascot Fleet at Duke's Palace in Norwich, late 1930s

Throughout the war, everyone suffered reductions, hardship and restrictions. Clothing coupons were introduced in June 1941. Having been trained as a seam-stress at F.W. Harmer and Co before she married, Hilda was very adept at making clothes for the children. She was   particularly good at making suits for the boys – all three of them. I should think the rompers and dresses were made from parachute silk.

Food was rationed as well but the WRVS held regular demonstrations to show how to make the most of limited supplies. Hilda was a very good cook and I remember one of her specialities was a good pot of beef stew with white fluffy dumplings.

Rationing did not worry the family too much; Leonard had many 'contacts' – black market or otherwise – who came in very useful for extras, including fuel for the coaches. Petrol was usually available because Leonard was carrying out essential war work by transporting workers to airfields to re-build runways.

Due to a weak heart, Leonard could not enter any of the armed services but nevertheless his work was considered very important for the war effort.

When not required for Government contracts, the coaches were used to transport the Votier family concert party to entertain the troops at the many R.A.F. and Army camps situated in remote corners in and around Norfolk – mostly under the cover of night. Possibly 200 – 300 camps were visited during the war years.

Leonard and Hilda sang – he was a tenor and she a very accomplished soprano. Daughters Stella and Eileen danced. Occasionally they were asked to transport members of the local E.N.S.A (which became jokingly called 'Every Night Something Awful) or officially known as the Army sponsored scheme, Entertainments National Services Association.

Entertainers, costumes and odd pieces of hastily built scenery would be taken along to the camps and the show would go ahead on a makeshift stage.

Many professional entertainers volunteered their services and one person of note was the late Mr. David Nixon, the magician. Leonard was often asked to assist Mr. Nixon with his tricks and he, being a practical joker, often messed them up.

Ted Votier with pal Roy Broom at Felthorpe

CHAPTER 6
A NEW HOUSE – A NEW BABY

During the spring of 1942, Norwich was a prime target for bombing by the Germans, and was bombed more than forty times. A lot of damage was caused during the BAEDEKER raids, with public houses, entertainment centres and hundreds of houses being destroyed. Some medieval churches were destroyed, including St. Paul's. The family home at 24 Magdalen Road was hit, with substantial damage to the ceilings and windows – it was time to move.

Leonard had spotted a house for sale on Cromer Road at Hellesdon, during one of the many visits to Felthorpe Woods. Being within close proximity to St. Faith's Airfield (now Norwich Airport) the price was very reasonable – no one wanted property close to an airfield in case the aircraft crashed, or it might have been a target for bombing, and that is why the price was so low. Paying the sum of £400, the purchase was completed and the family moved in. In March 1943 Jill Andrea Votier – the author – was born.

It was a pleasant house with a long drive up to the front door, opening on to a long entrance hall. There was a lounge, separate sitting room with French doors out to the long rear garden. The kitchen had a walk-in pantry and internal coal house, and there was also an integral garage. The stair-case led up to four bedrooms and the bathroom. Coal fires heated the downstairs rooms and in the winter we scraped the ice off the inside of the window panes in our bedrooms.

Also at this time, Leonard was looking for new premises for the coaches. He acquired a piece of land at the junction of Mile Cross Lane and Vulcan Road South. Bob Bush, a local builder did the main brickwork for the garage and Messrs. Dorneys did the steelwork.

It was a large building with heavy steel-clad sliding doors on the Mile Cross Lane frontage. There were nine bays to house the coaches side-by-side.
This arrangement was preferred so the coaches could easily be manoeuvred and moved out in case of fire. There was a long inspection pit at one end, often used by the Ministry for large vehicle inspections.

Garage at Mile Cross Lane

Coach Repairs
In the early 1950s, repairs to the coaches were carried out by the family. In the event of a breakdown or damage to a coach, a driver would ring in on his way back from a journey. Leonard would put his clothes over his pyjamas and light a cigarette – he chain smoked in those days. He would then go to the garage in Mile Cross Lane with the two older boys, Lenny and Ted.

Most body work repairs were easy to carry out – the coaches had metal panels over a wooden frame in most cases, so the damaged panel could be removed and a new one put in its place. They would sometimes work all night to get the coach ready for the next day's job.

For engine repairs John Loom - Stores Manager at Delves Motors – would turn out anytime of night or day to find the part required.

As the coaches became more sophisticated, part-time fitters were used at night times. These included Arnold Read, an auto electrician, and Wally Nickerson. They were all experienced on Bedford Coaches.

Leonard was always keen to keep his hand in at driving the coaches. Once a year we had a family outing, usually at the end of the season when there were fewer excursions. Members of the family, respective partners and children would board the coach and the driver would set off to what was supposed to be a mystery tour and secret destination. We all knew we would end up in Felixstowe as usual, but kept up the pretence of an adventure for the children.

On one such outing in 1956, after enjoying a morning on the beach, we walked over the road to Cordy's restaurant where we had a fish-and-chip lunch in the upstairs restaurant. Later that afternoon, Leonard announced he would be driving the coach back to Norwich himself.

Imagine the scene when, on leaving Felixstowe, he negotiated a roundabout the wrong way round; the last time Leonard drove down that road the roundabout had not been constructed. After a bit of heckling from the rear of the coach, Leonard decided to leave the driving to the experts after that.

By the late 1940s the coaches were sometimes used for more social and family outings. At the beginning of the school holidays a coach would be packed with bedding, clothes, food, toys and games, plus the three youngest children Bill, Judy and Jill. We were allowed to take along a school friend and would set off early evening for the family bungalow in California Avenue in Scratby.

En route the highlight of the day was calling for fish and chips – in paper – at the wooden hut on Ormesby Green.

We would remain at the bungalow for the month of August. Mrs. Davis, an excellent cook, was chaperone once but the regular housekeeper was Mrs. Barnard who kept an eye on the youngsters; she made excellent curries and Mr. Barnard did the garden.

Other families spending their holidays in the area were the Sewell girls from Acle, the Allen boys from Desborough and the Jephcotts who came from Leicester. Neighbours at Scratby were other local business families, the Braceys and Purdys.

Leonard and Hilda would visit on a Sunday afternoon. The days were spent swimming; both in the sea and at the open air swimming pool at Great Yarmouth. We attended many 'galas' at the baths in which brother Bill often took part, followed by a game of water polo. These days were really happy, lazy, crazy times. The older children of the family – now married with children of their own – would spend their annual holidays at the bungalow named 'MASCOT'.

One of the regular drivers at this time was Billy Walker. He came from the London area and so drove the coaches to London on a regular basis. His son, Jim Walker, told me Billy was allowed to take his coach home at night as he would have an early morning start – it took five hours to get to London in those days.

Whilst his father was resting, Jim and his brother would sweep out the coach in readiness for the journey the next day. Sometimes they found the odd sixpence and this kept them in sweets for the week. Needless to say, they were always very keen to help out.

Some of the drivers who worked for Mascot were:

Billy Walker
Arthur Youell
Donnie and Reggie Paveley
Stanley Crane
Harry Backlog ('Bootlace')
Jack Reeve
Charlie Miller
George Summers
'Digby'
'Dingy Bell'
Neil Stansbury
Bill Smith
Jock Salter
Ernie Harvey (who always sucked Murray Mints!)
Richard Grout
Les Asplin

They were proud to wear their long white coats in the early days, but when the company expanded with the takeovers, they wore maroon blazers with the cathedral emblem embroidered in gold thread on the breast pocket. The maroon ties had the same emblem on them.

This uniform was finished off with crisp white shirts, grey flannel trousers and black shoes – very smart, and well turned out as well.

An outing from the Clarke Road area of Norwich c.1945. Leonard is on the far right.

CHAPTER 7
THE MANN EGERTON CONNECTION

Whilst researching material for this book, it soon became apparent to me that there was a strong connection between Mascot and Mann Egerton. I thought it would be interesting to find out a little more about this company.

Gerard Noel Cornwallis Mann was a Cornishman and electrical engineer. In April 1899 he saw an advertisement detailing a Norwich electrical installation business for sale. He subsequently purchased the firm from Laurence Scott and Co.

Hubert Wingfield Egerton, born in 1875, was the son of a rector at Weston Longville, Norfolk.

The two men met during 1900 and decided to set up business as partners. Their first premises were at Prince of Wales Road, Norwich. They were primarily involved with engineering work and then aircraft for use in World War I.

In 1915, using a war loan of £30,000 they acquired 60 acres of open land at Cromer Road, Norwich. They built three large wooden hangars parallel with Cromer Road, reaching almost to Heather Avenue. These hangars were ultimately used to house parts and components for coachbuilding.

Mann Egerton built coaches for the then popular 'seaside excursions' which the public were demanding. A family friend of ours, Arthur Braithwaite, was one of the first apprentices Mann Egerton took on after World War II. He was a trainee coachbuilder, working his way up to Assistant Works Manager, a position he held until 1964.

Keith Rackham joined the company in 1947 at the age of 14 as a trainee coachbuilder. He worked for two years as a shop boy and then five years as an apprentice.

The drawing office took up half the balcony space in the coachbuilding hangar. The windows overlooked Cromer Road, almost opposite the family home at No. 68. On the inner side of the office was a full size drawing board. My brother-in-law, Brian Marston, who married my sister Eileen, worked as a draughtsman. Brian designed the ash wood body for a 29 seater Austin coach. This was the only one actually built from scratch, another one was completely stripped out and re-built there.

29 seater coach ex. Mann Egerton c.1947

My oldest sister, Stella also worked for Mann Egerton's. She was Secretary for the Sports and Social Club. In 1946 she organised the firm's annual outing to London. A convoy of Mascot Coaches were used to transport some 300 passengers to London for the day.

Mann Egerton works' outing, 21st September 1946

*Bob Rowlands at Mann Egerton works
by the shell of a 29 seater coach*

Mann Egerton became specialist coachbuilders. The chassis would be purchased from the manufacturers – I can remember seeing these strange looking vehicles with the driver at the front very warmly dressed in helmets, goggles and leather jackets to protect them from the elements, constantly being driven into the factory. The customers would then discuss the coachwork – nothing was mass produced in those days.

Another family friend, George Robert Webb, a sheet metal worker and panel beater also worked for Mann Egerton's. He would carefully shape and create curved pieces of metal for the backs and fronts of the coaches. An apprentice panel beater who learnt his trade from 'Pop' Webb was Bob 'Taffy' Rowlands of Aylsham.

In the 1950s, handbuilt coaches were getting rather expensive for Mascot, and Leonard decided to buy direct from the manufacturers. The main suppliers were Duples of Ware in Hertfordshire and W.S. Yeates Ltd of Loughborough.

I can remember when each new coach was brought to the house in Cromer Road. Mother and all of us children would be invited to get on board and we were driven along Cromer Road, Fifer's Lane and back along Mile Cross Lane. Leonard was proud to show off his newest acquisition.

CHAPTER 8
BUSINESS BOOMED

Between 1948-1958 business boomed for Mascot, as coach travel was much in demand. People started to go out more and factories, public houses, clubs and works had their annual outings.

The driver would load up crates of beer, ginger beer and lemonade and perhaps a box of Smith's crisps. On the homeward journey the driver would pull into a lay-by. The passengers would then line up at the back of the coach and share out the refreshments. Back on the coach, passengers would break into song and there were frequent 'comfort' stops. There were no modern services areas then, just a hedge or tree had to do for anyone needing to 'spend a penny'.

Mascot was a private enterprise coach firm providing a much-needed public service. Some of the contract work they were involved in included:

Wednesday and Sunday services from Norwich to Kelling Sanatorium. This was started by Leonard as a service to the community rather than a commercial undertaking by the firm. It ran for 35 years. The family also had a long association with the Friends of Kelling.

Regular holiday period return services to Butlin's holiday camps at Clacton and Skegness on Saturdays.

Outings of all kinds for local organisations including Old Folks' Clubs, Royal British Legion, Darts, Norwich Rugby Club and The Estates Bowls Club.

Many factory outings, state school contracts during term time. I think I was the only pupil at Lonsdale School on Earlham Road who was collected from school by a coach instead of a car. Together with two or three friends from the Hellesdon area, we would rattle home in a smart 45-seater. One driver, Harry Backlog, loved to take us home via Mile Cross Bridge –

An outing from the Falcon Public House, c. 1947   Photo courtesy of Eastern Counties Newspapers

he would accelerate over the bridge just to hear us shout as our stomachs dropped.

The Post Office hired coaches at Christmas time to cope with the increased amount of parcels. It was a strange sight to see all sizes of brown paper packages tied up with string and sealing wax, on the seats where passengers normally sat.

The Home Office hired coaches to transport prisoners to and from Norwich Prison and the courts. A Home Office warden was always in attendance and the prisoners were handcuffed to them and also to the rail on the back of the seats – to my knowledge they never lost a prisoner!

On Saturday evenings, coaches transported young ladies from Norwich to R.A.F. Sculthorpe, near Fakenham, which at that time was an American air base. The ladies would be attending social functions and dances laid on by the American service men, and one driver, Charlie Miller, remembered the girls changing out of their work clothes into their finery while en route – observed by a driver's carefully adjusted rear-view mirror.

Although security was very strict by the American Military police, some coaches returned to Norwich only half full.

Luxury coaches of all sizes were provided for away matches for the Norwich City Supporter's Club. Leonard was President of this club from 1955 – 1961.

The pride of the fleet, in its full livery of maroon and champagne, was a Bedford with a Duple body Reg. No. HPW 707D. This would normally have been a 41 seater coach. However, it was the Norwich City Football Club team coach, so it had 2 pairs of seat removed and replaced by tables and the corresponding seats faced backwards thus making it a 37 seater.

Mascot were heavily involved in the F.A. cup run of 1959. Leonard hired coaches from all the firms in the area to meet the huge demand for seats. The A11 was a sea of yellow and green as fans waved their scarves out of the coach windows.

With the opening of the University of East Anglia at Earlham in the late 1960s, Mascot secured the contract to provide an express bus service for 650 students from their living quarters at Fifer's Lane to the U.E.A. – a distance of some 4.8 miles, and this took 12 minutes. Mascot was well placed to run this service as the depot at Vulcan Road was close to the residences.

The University service required 2 coaches daily which ran at approximately 30 minute intervals from 09.30 to 23.15 during term time.

The service was operated under contract to the University and they were responsible for collecting the fares. Students mostly purchased season tickets but single tickets were available from the porter's lodge. In the main, Mascot drivers did not check tickets, only occasionally they would have a purge and eject any students without tickets.

Panks Outing c. 1960. Photo by kind permission of Roy Burton

Panks Outing

My thanks to Roy Burton who told me that when the firm had their annual works outing, they left The Hippodrome Theatre in St. Giles Street, Norwich at about 7a.m. The first stop would be somewhere near Barton Mills in a lay-by for refreshments.

The driver would then proceed to the outskirts of North London to stop at a hotel for a mid-day meal. Around 2pm, they would travel to see a first division football match and after tea at 7.30pm they would go on to a London show, possibly The Crazy Gang starring Flannegan and Allen.

By 11pm they would meet at the 'White Bear' restaurant in Piccadily Circus for an evening meal and then depart for Norwich around 1.30am, stopping on the way at Red Lodge at Frettenham, arriving back at Norwich about 6am – a good day out!

Some coaches used at this time were:

1953 Bedford SB3 Burlingham	Reg no ONG 102
1956 Bedford SB3 Super Duple Vega	Reg No UAH 102
1960 Bedford SB1 Duple Vega	Reg No 7102 AH

*Leonard (centre)
with pals Ernie Page
(left) and Jack Scott
(right)*

Norwich Lads' Club visit to Leeuwarden, Holland.

Chapter 9
End of an era

Leonard Votier always worked hard, he was very popular and a great family man. The family was devastated on 16th April, 1961 when he died, very suddenly, at the age of 59 years.

Not only had he been a keen business man, he also played a prominent part in the sporting, social and local government life in Norwich and the surrounding district.

Many tributes poured in after his death and words such

Leonard Votier
1902 - 1961

as kind, helpful, sympathetic, practical, friendly, warm hearted, generous and with a real sense of humour were repeated many times.

In the next Norwich City Football Club Handbook, the tribute to their late president ended, "His passing is a great tragedy to us all and we know that through the years to come we shall often hear the phrase 'If only Len had been here'."

It was encouraging to know he was held in great esteem by so many but to me, the youngest child, he was a lovely man with a pleasant, kind personality – he was MY DAD.

The coach business was left to my mother Hilda and, with the help of my brothers Lenny, Ted and Bill it was carried on as before. The head office at that time was situated on Vulcan Road, behind the garage at Mile Cross Lane. The company continued to prosper and expand and

from a turnover of £18,000 in 1961, grew to a turnover of £200,000 in 1973. This mainly came about after the company went limited and bought out several smaller firms around Norfolk.

These included:
Allens of Reepham.
Green and Grey of Cromer
(founded by R. Babbage and Son in 1919).
Seagull Felix and Grangeways
(secured from James Calver of Great Yarmouth).
Private hire work and one coach of Carley Motors
of Fakenham.
Three coaches owned by Kent of Alborough.

Following these take-overs, MASCOT became the largest privately owned coach firm in the area, offering a wide range of coaches with approximately 1500 seats available for hire.

Continental tours were on offer from the early 1960s. MASCOT offered a unique door-to-door service with own coach throughout the journey. By the early 70s the company had extended their tours to Holland, France, Belgium and Germany. A typical tour to Holland would commence at 7.a.m. from Bell Avenue in Norwich. After the driver had stowed away the luggage in the rear of the coach they would set off for Harwich to cross the North Sea on the 'Princess Juliana'. By early evening, the party settled in a hotel at Scheveningham on the Dutch coast. Once there, the party would enjoy an eight day tour for £38 all in. Another destination was Switzerland, where it was possible to travel to Lucerne for 11 days at a cost of £75. A similar trip in 2005 would cost you around £500.

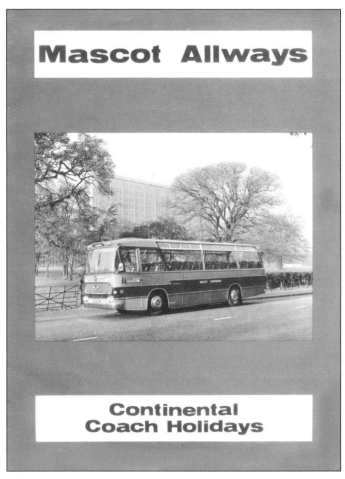

County Hall in Norwich provided the backdrop for this brochure

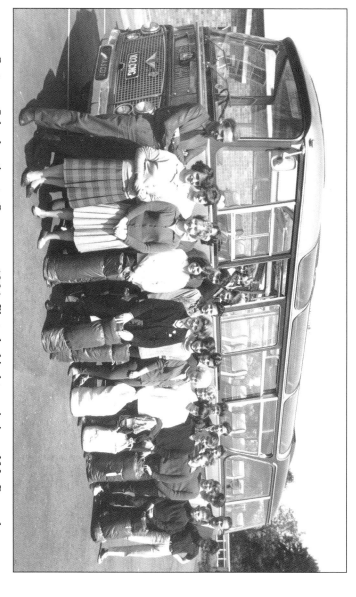

Costessey School outing to Germany c.1964. Photo by kind permission of Mr. Peacock

In the early 1970s Hilda lost most of her eyesight. But, as she always maintained that you do not need to see to answer the telephone, that is what she did, and she continued to make daily visits to the office. At the age of 70 she could still work out quotations, answer queries and sort out everyday problems, something she had done throughout her married life whilst bringing up seven children, at the same time being actively involved in many clubs and charitable organisations in and around Norwich.

On 18th March, 1975 it was time for Hilda to retire. Most of the business had been sold off by then when MASCOT merged with Eastern Counties Omnibus Company and all coach holidays, charter work and excursions were operated under the title of Mascot National. Mascot Seagull of Great Yarmouth continued for a couple more years under the Votier family control until it was eventually wound up. The name MASCOT was never sold.

Hilda May Votier, 1904 – 1976
Photograph by Johnson Taylor, Elm Hill, Norwich

Sadly, the family was once more devastated when Hilda died in December 1976. She was MY MUM, a hard-working businesswoman, charity worker and friend to all. She certainly lived a very full and active life and loved, and was loved, by her children, grandchildren and great grandchildren.

Hilda Votier with family, taken in 1969.
(Photo courtesy of Eastern Daily Press).

After Mascot ceased trading, Hilda's sons followed their own careers.

Leonard Owen (Lenny) Votier *(back row, second left)* was employed as departmental Manager for Tricentrol in Mountgate, Norwich. After a long illness, sadly he passed away on 26th February, 1998.

William Edward (Ted) Votier *(front row, third right)* worked as a marine engineer in a boatyard at Wroxham. Ted endured a long illness and passed away on 22nd November, 1989.

Malcolm Reginald (Bill) Votier *(back row, second right)* joined Amoco at their Bacton Gas Site as a technician. Later he helped his wife Rosemary to run their boarding house at Cromer. Bill died suddenly at his home on 17th August, 2004 after suffering a heart attack.

All are fondly remembered, may they rest in peace.

CHAPTER 10
HOBBIES AND CHARITY WORK

Although their free time was very limited with the work involved in the business and their family, Leonard and Hilda were very mindful of the needs of others and gave a great deal of this time, and their energy, to charity work.

Leonard and Hilda were particularly interested in the welfare of the elderly. Their involvement with the E.N.S.A concert parties during the war years gave them an added interest in entertaining.

At Christmas time they would visit Old Folks' Clubs and help to organise party games. The favourites always seemed to include Pass the Parcel, Nelson's Eye, Musical Chairs and the Blarney Stone. Prizes were given for the winners and these were usually Cadbury 'penny' chocolate bars.

The parties would always end with a few songs from Hilda and Leonard, when they were accompanied on the piano by Hilda's sister, Betty Lincoln.

Some of the clubs which they visited included:
    St. Barnabas.
    Park Lane Over 65 Club
    Hellesdon Old Folks Club
    Lewis Buckingham Club for Old People
    Various M.A.G.N.A. Clubs.

In 1941 a campaign was organised in Norwich for a band of women to set up a scheme of mutual aid to assist air-raid victims. This was intended to be in co-operation with the A.R.P., Civil Defence and other voluntary organisations. It was given the name of the Mutual Aid Good Neighbours Association, or M.A.G.N.A. for short.

Mrs. Ruth Hardy was the organiser for Norwich and Hilda and Leonard became involved from the early stages through their A.R.P. work.

M.A.G.N.A. provided warmth, shelter, sympathy and kindness, and members ran whist drives, concerts and dances to raise funds. Hilda and Leonard often welcomed members into their home.

The first M.A.G.N.A Club was opened in Northumberland Street, Norwich and in the early 1960s the Votier family helped to raise over £1,000 for a further club to be built in Little Bull Close, Norwich. That club opened on 7th December 1962 after Leonard's death. Hilda remained President until her death in 1976.

Hilda and Leonard also played a part in local government, as councillors on the St. Faiths and Aylsham Rural District Council (later to become Broadland Council) and their local Hellesdon Parish Council (1956-1961).

They also took an interest in local education and sat on the governing bodies at Sprowston Secondary Modern School and Hellesdon Secondary Modern School. In later years Hilda took an interest in the Broadland Secondary Modern School as well as Thorpe Grammar School.

Through his connections in transport, Leonard was a long- serving committee member for Norwich Traffic Club and served as a community service committee member for Norwich Rotary Club from 1953 to 1961. Hilda was a member of the Norwich Inner Wheel Club.

Both Hilda and Leonard enjoyed working with the Royal British Legion and Hilda was President of the Mile Cross ladies Section for many years.

Leonard was captain of the Church Lads' Brigade at St. Clement's Church in Norwich. The photograph below shows members of the Lads' Brigade outside Buckingham Palace in 1938. Leonard can be seen in his smart uniform on the far left.

Leonard's favourite pastime was playing outdoor bowls. He spent many happy hours at the Estates Green on Aylsham Road and the Falcon Public House Green on Cromer Road. He occasionally played for Norfolk Bowls Club on Unthank Road, and was President for the Estates and City League Clubs. His constant bowling pals were Benny Laws and Jack Scott.

Leonard also enjoyed game shooting during the winter months at the Quidenham Estate. He was in a syndicate there with Jack Scott. Hilda often entertained members of the shooting parties at their home in Cromer Road, Hellesdon and one person of note who was a frequent house guest, was Lord Strabolgi, an M.P.

Estates Bowling Club, Mile Cross c.1953
Leonard Votier is on the back row, 2nd left

The family had a huge interest in the Friends of
Kelling, a group which was formed in 1948 by three
former patients of the hospital – Jack Thomas, Fred
Clabour and Geoffrey McEwen.

They set out to provide extra amenities for long-stay
patients at this tuberculosis hospital near Holt, in
Norfolk.

The committee approached Leonard regarding
transportation for visitors from Norwich to the hospital
and for many years he subsidised travel. The service
operated three times a week. In the 1950s the hospital
consisted of three large areas – a male wing, female
wing and a children's section.

Both Leonard and Hilda were members of the
general council which had the Chief Constable of
Norwich, Alan Plume, as President.

An annual appeal fund was set up and funds raised
were used to provide transport for concert parties,
who went along to entertain the patients, plus outings
to the sea-side at Cromer followed by high tea for the
children.

Also, the annual Christmas Party for the children, which was always attended by the Lord Mayor elect of Norwich, along with other civic dignitaries.

Father Christmas made a grand entrance on these occasions driving down the long drive to the hospital on a sleigh, weighed down with gifts for all the children.

To mark Leonard's passing, Hilda provided two oak bench seats for the long driveway to the male hospital so that patients, and visitors could stop for a rest. The provision of a Day Ward at Home Place Convalescent Home prompted Hilda to donate an oak writing desk for use by the patients.

In 1969, the Lord Mayor of Norwich hosted a Civic Reception at Norwich Castle Keep to mark the 21st anniversary of the Friends of Kelling. To mark the occasion Hilda made a large fruit cake which was professionally iced. Several members of the VOTIER family were guests at this magnificent evening.

A keen and loyal fan of Norwich City Football Club, Leonard was a shareholder and a season ticket holder. He was president of the Norwich City Football Supporter's Club from 1955 to 1961. A very moving experience for the family, which showed the affection held for Leonard, was the wearing of black armbands by the Norwich Team for their first match after his death and a minute's silence which was held by all present before the match.

Through their love of football, Leonard and Hilda were keen supporters of the Norwich Schools Football Association. This Association was formed in 1897 when local competitions and school shield matches provided the only competitive soccer for all grades of schoolboys. The team were known as the 'Norwich Boys'.

In the 1947/48 season, after playing 14 games, the 'boys' reached the semi-final. In this year Leonard and Hilda presented the 'MASCOT CUP' as a mark of appreciation for the achievements of the 'boys'. This cup was played for on each Good Friday at the Carrow Road ground between the Norwich Boys and a team chosen from those they had played during the season. The match was followed by a very well received high tea.

A regular 'Norwich Boy' – Malcolm Howard of Newton Flotman – recalls the year 1948, when he was a lad of 15. He was chosen by his school – The Norman School in Norwich – to join the Boys for the Mascot Cup game, when the opposing team was from West Ham. Malcolm had fond memories of Leonard, who often drove the coaches to their away matches.

On one particular occasion they were all taken to see a London Show 'Flannegan and Allen' and stayed overnight at the County Hotel. Malcolm remembered that there was no charge made to the boys for the coach travel, show or hotel. These generous actions by Leonard were very much appreciated by all, especially as this was shortly after the war and people did not have cash to spend on entertainment.

The Mascot Cup competition was a regular feature until 1965 and then the cup seemed to vanish. In 1999 the family decided to make serious enquiries about the possible whereabouts of the Mascot Cup, and with the help of the Radio Norfolk Helpline it was discovered in the trophy cabinet at Sprowston High School. Nobody seemed to know how it had arrived there, or indeed how long it had even been there. It was in a rather sorry state of repair with the base missing, which was a great shame as this held the small shields bearing the names of all the teams who had won the cup. Also missing was the lid of the cup which held a solid silver model of a boy footballer.

However, it was still a magnificent trophy and the VOTIER family had the cup renovated, modified and cleaned. Despite several attempts nobody seemed willing to take on the cup again for the boy's football, but the Norfolk School's Football Association, represented by Stuart Dracup, were delighted to accept this trophy for the Girls Under 14 competition. In 2001, the first Mascot Cup League Competition for Under 14 Girls took place and on 7th March the worthy winners were a team from the Hewett High School, Norwich. It was a very emotional, and proud, moment for the members of the VOTIER family who were able to be present on that day.

It is the hope of all the family that this competition will continue for many years and will carry on the tradition started by Leonard and Hilda many years ago, to encourage young people to take part in competitive sport.

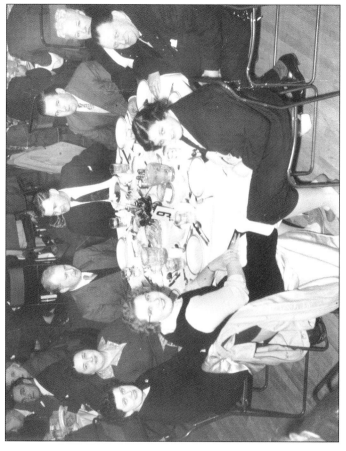

The Votier family at Norwich Rotary Club family luncheon, 1956

MY MUM AND DAD

A tribute by Jill Howard

Len and Hilda Votier were my mum and dad;
When they died it made me very sad.
Dad was born in 1902 and mum in 1904
They had seven children then there was me –
one more.

Dad left school at quite an early age.
Not much of a scholar, about average for his age.
His very first job was making boots and shoes
This wasn't quite his scene, he was unable to choose.

The next profession of a motor car driver.
He was still engaged in when he met my mother.
She was the daughter of the Nelsons of Heigham
They were wed in December and a new life they began.

Their first house was at Great Yarmouth,
62 Admiralty Road.
Dad drove a fish van then – I have been told.
Their first child, Leonard, was born in this town
Christened at St. Nicholas's which was later
bombed down.

Some time later, to Norwich they did move.
Dad carried on driving and this was his love.
He carted many bricks for re-building schemes
Of owning a charabanc he often did dream.

His step-father William, surname of Fake.
Made him an offer he really should take.
He put up the money for a fine shiny roadster
Dad took delivery and then he was the master.

All through the war years they worked very hard
Building up the business and acquiring a yard.
They opened an office in old Magdalen Street
Sometimes mother was run off her feet.

Despite the hard work, they had time for fun
Coaches to Kelling sanatorium my dad did run.
They always helped people not so well off as they
Air-raid wardens, entertainers – just part of their days.

They organised parties in Old People's Clubs.
Dad played darts in many local pubs.
They both belonged to the Royal British Legion
Dad enjoyed watching Norwich City F.C. for many
a season

They once owned a bungalow at Scratby by the sea.
That was a nice place where the family liked to be.
Many a school holiday found all us kids there
With school friends and family, happy times we
did share.

Mum and dad lived many years in a house at Hellesdon.
Their work in society was very welcome.
They helped raise funds for the local community
centre
Attending fetes and fairs in all kinds of weather.

The coach firm thrived for some fifty years.
It brought much enjoyment, sometimes a few tears
It all came to an end in nineteen seventy-three
But the name MASCOT will 'ALLWAYS' remain with me.